Get to Work with Science and Technology

The Wonderful Worlds of a
Video Game Designer

by Ruth Owen

Consultant:

Will Freeman
Video game journalist and consultant

Ruby Tuesday Books

Published in 2016 by Ruby Tuesday Books Ltd.

Editor: Mark J. Sachner
Designer: Emma Randall
Production: John Lingham

Photo Credits:
Alamy: 5 (top), 9 (left), 10, 14 (top), 21 (bottom), 27 (top), 28; Corbis: 4, 9 (top), 29; Getty Images: 6, 7; Oliver Hollis: 16; Istock Photo: 19 (top right); Press Association Images: 21 (top); Public Domain: 8, 9 (right); Ruby Tuesday Books: 7 (top); Shutterstock: Cover, 2–3, 5 (center: Oleg Doroshin), 5 (bottom), 11, 12–13, 14, 15, 18 (left: 3 Song Photography), 18 (right), 19 (top left), 19 (bottom), 20 (small1), 22–23, 26, 27 (bottom: Konstantin Sutyagin), 30; Superstock: 17; Unity Technologies: 12 (bottom), 24–25.

Library of Congress Control Number: 2015940234

ISBN 978-1-910549-32-2

Printed and published in the United States of America

For further information including rights and permissions requests, please contact our Customer Service Department at 877-337-8577.

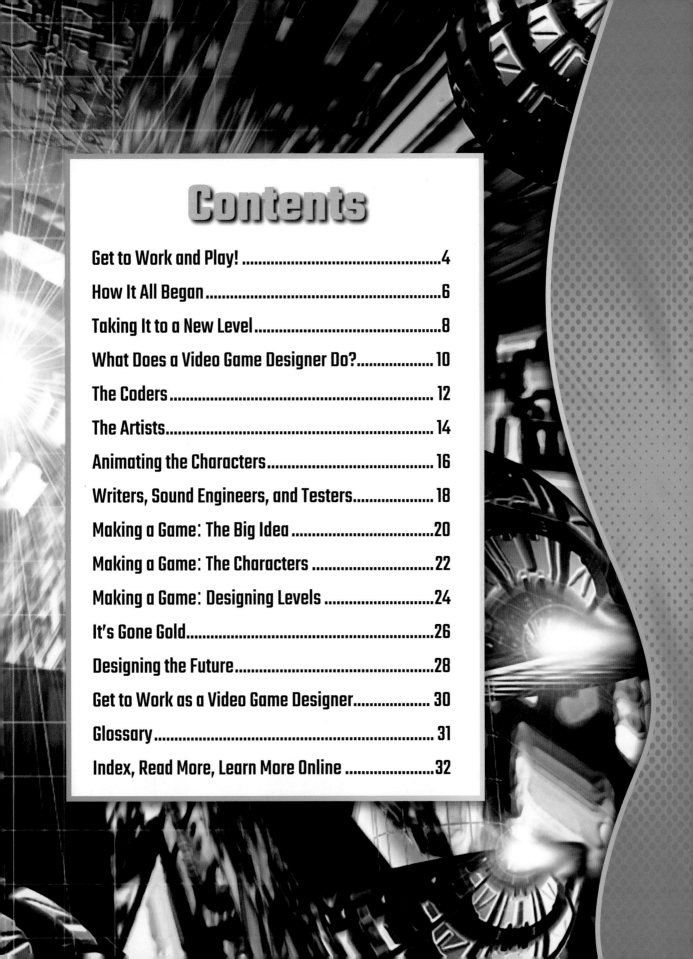

Contents

Get to Work and Play! 4

How It All Began 6

Taking It to a New Level 8

What Does a Video Game Designer Do?.................. 10

The Coders 12

The Artists.. 14

Animating the Characters... 16

Writers, Sound Engineers, and Testers.................... 18

Making a Game: The Big Idea 20

Making a Game: The Characters 22

Making a Game: Designing Levels 24

It's Gone Gold..26

Designing the Future..28

Get to Work as a Video Game Designer.................. 30

Glossary... 31

Index, Read More, Learn More Online 32

Get to Work and Play!

It's just one minute to midnight. In a crowded shopping mall, thousands of excited video game fans are waiting. Tonight, a new action-adventure game will be launched.

Maybe you're in the line, eager to play the new game. Or maybe you've already played it—hundreds and hundreds of times. That's because you're the designer, or developer, of this soon-to-be hit game. Sound like a cool dream for the future?

It doesn't have to just be a dream. The video game **industry** is big business. This means if you love playing games and have good computer skills or lots of creativity, you might one day get to work as a video game designer.

Excited video game fans wait in line at a launch event.

Players of *Minecraft* and *The Sims* use their creativity to build whole worlds. These students are creating scenes from the novel *The Hobbit* in *Minecraft*.

Action, sports, driving, role-playing—there are many different **genres**, or types, of video games. In role-playing games, such as *World of Warcraft*, players control a character **avatar** and go on quests and solve puzzles.

Today, games are designed for smartphones, tablets, PCs, and consoles, such as Xboxes and PlayStations.

How It All Began

The first video games were created by **computer scientists** more than 60 years ago.

In those days, computers were enormous, room-sized machines. Only a small number of scientists knew how to **program** and use them.

In 1951, a British company named Ferranti built a game-playing computer called NIMROD. The computer was built for a science exhibition in London. At the exhibition, visitors got the chance to play a counting and **strategy** game against the computer. The game was called *Nim*.

NIMROD's creators didn't design the game so people could have fun. They wanted to show the world that it was possible to program a computer to do math calculations.

NIMROD computer

Game display

INSTRUCTION

Control panel

The NIMROD computer was 5 feet (1.5 m) tall, 12 feet (3.7 m) wide, and 9 feet (2.7 m) deep.

The *OXO* game screen

The EDSAC computer

In 1952, British computer scientist Alexander S. Douglas developed a computerized game of tic-tac-toe, called *OXO*. The game was played on a computer called the EDSAC. A person played *OXO* against the computer.

The EDSAC (Electronic Delay Storage Automatic Calculator) was built by scientists at the University of Cambridge in England.

Taking It to a New Level

In 1962, a team of computer scientists at the Massachusetts Institute of Technology (MIT) designed a two-player game called *Spacewar!* As the players tried to shoot their opponent's spaceship, they had to avoid being sucked into a star. To play the game, the team built control boxes from scraps of wood and wire, and odd bits of electrical equipment. *Spacewar!* was designed to show what a computer could do. It also showed that computer games could be a lot of fun!

Worldwide, computer scientists got to work building computers and developing games. By the 1980s, video game fans were playing games at **video arcades**.

Spacewar! was one of the first video games to look and play like the games we enjoy today.

Video game players in an arcade in 1982

At video arcades, players enjoyed games such as *Space Invaders* and *Pac-Man*. People played some games standing at upright cabinets. Other games were played on table-like machines that had a small screen in the tabletop.

A *Space Invaders* game from 1980

By the 1990s, games were played on home consoles and handheld devices such as the Nintendo Game Boy.

Nintendo Game Boy

What Does a Video Game Designer Do?

Today there are hundreds of thousands of video games. Whether the player is mining and crafting, matching candy shapes, or fighting mutant creatures, it's the designer who comes up with a game's idea.

The designer decides on the game's rules, the player's **objectives**, the **levels**, and the look of the game. Some games have just one designer, while others have many designers working together.

Once a designer has an idea, he or she may then work with a development team. The team will include **coders**, or programmers, artists, writers, sound engineers, and testers. Each team member has a role to play in making the designer's idea come to life.

Video game designer Jaakko Iisalo created the mobile app game *Angry Birds*.

A designer's idea might be an action game that plays for 10 hours or more.

It might be a mobile game that can be played in just five minutes.

It's possible for one person working alone to create a successful video game. Some games, however, are created by a team of up to 1,000 people!

The Coders

The development team members who write a video game's **code** are the coders, or programmers. When you make your character run, or a door in a haunted house slowly opens and creaks, it's the game's code that makes this happen.

Coders also write the code to create a game's **artificial intelligence (AI)**. These are the parts of the game where the game must think for itself. The game's AI decides how many zombies will stagger toward you. It also decides how the groaning undead will act when you wave a flaming torch at them. An action game with realistic **3D (three-dimensional)** images may have up to 3 million lines of code!

Many games are built using a "game engine." Game engines are computer tools that can be used to connect the coding, art, and sounds that make up a game. The engine powers the game and helps it run, like an engine in a car.

A game engine running on a game designer's screen. It shows the game being made.

The code to make the worm move around the square looks like this.

```
for (var count = 0; count < 4; count++) {
  moveForward(100);
  turnRight(90);
}
```

Coders do all their work on computers using special code-writing **software**. Writing video game code is complicated and difficult. To do this job, a person needs strong computer science and math skills.

The Artists

A video game designer imagines how a game will look. Then a team of artists creates a world of characters and **environments** out of the designer's ideas.

Concept Artists

Concept artists are the first artists to work on a new game. They make hundreds of rough pencil sketches, detailed colored drawings, or pieces of digital art. Their work helps the team understand how the characters, environments, and game world will look. Once the designer is happy, character artists and environment artists take over.

Character Artists

Character artists turn the concept artist's ideas into 2D or 3D characters. To create a 3D character, an artist makes a rough shape of the character with modeling software. Next, using shapes called polygons, the artist creates a more detailed model. Finally, the artist adds skin, fur, clothes, armor, and other details to the model.

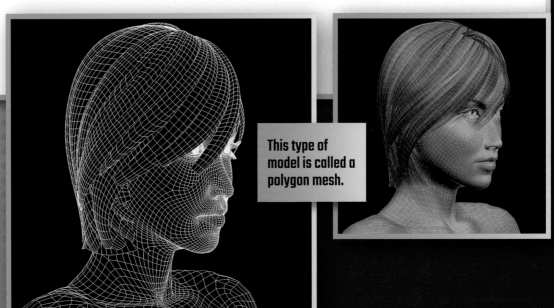

This type of model is called a polygon mesh.

Character artists use the real world for **inspiration**. For example, they might study military uniforms to create an outfit for a soldier. A crocodile's skin might be the inspiration for the scales on a dragon.

Environment artists add colors and textures, such as rock and metal, to their models. They do this by using programs such as Photoshop.

Environment Artists

Environment artists also use the concept artist's ideas to create a world for the game. From alien planets to abandoned cities, spooky graveyards to medieval dungeons, they create the game's backgrounds. Environment artists use modeling programs to build the game's scenery.

Animating the Characters

The characters in a video game must run, jump, and perform lots of other actions. Making the characters move is called **animation**.

One way to animate 3D characters is to use real people in a process called motion capture, or mocap. To do this, an actor usually puts on a skin-tight black suit and cap. Small markers that look like balls are attached to the actor's outfit.

The actor carries out the game's actions. Cameras record the actor from every angle and pick up signals from the markers. On a computer, the signals are used to create a 3D digital skeleton that carries out the actor's movements. Artists called animators then combine the moving digital skeleton with the 3D model of the game's character.

The markers are positioned on parts of the body that move and bend, such as elbows, knees, and hands.

Motion capture suit

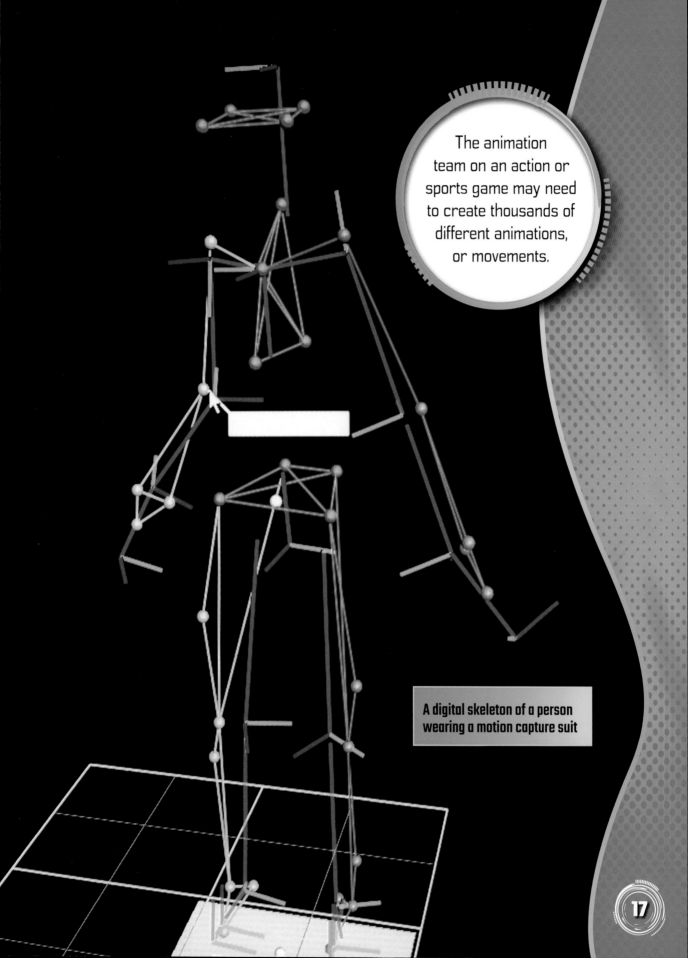

The animation team on an action or sports game may need to create thousands of different animations, or movements.

A digital skeleton of a person wearing a motion capture suit

Writers, Sound Engineers, and Testers

The other members of a video game development team may include a writer, sound engineers, and testers.

Video Game Writer

A writer helps develop a game's story. A video game designer may want to set her game in an abandoned, ruined city. The player has to move around the city and dodge mutant humans. Why is the city ruined, though? How did the people become mutants? And why are they after the player? The writer works with the designer to create this story.

An actor reading from a script

Sound Engineers

Sound engineers produce the music we hear when we play games. They also create a game's **sound effects**. Sound engineers might record real sounds to use, such as footsteps crunching on glass. They also use computer programs to create sounds such as swords clashing or moaning mutants.

A sound engineer using a mixing desk to work on the music for a video game.

Most video game writers also develop the dialogue, or words, for the game's characters. Then actors are recorded speaking the characters' words. The actors' voices are then added to the game.

A video game tester

Testers

Before a new game can be released and sold, it must be played and tested hundreds of times. This is the work of video game testers. A tester plays a game to find bugs—parts of the game that don't work. Then the tester reports the problems back to the coders so they can be fixed.

Making a Game: The Big Idea

So you want to create a video game. But where do game designers get their ideas from?

You can be inspired by reading books and magazines, and watching movies. Playing board games might inspire you, too. The neighborhood where you live, a lesson at school, or your hobbies can all give you ideas.

Video game designer Satoshi Tajiri created the world of *Pokémon*. As a child, Tajiri's hobby was collecting insects to study them. This hobby inspired Tajiri to create his game in which players collect Pokémon creatures.

A giant balloon in the shape of the Pikachu character from Pokémon

Fans of *World of Warcraft* play the game at a video games event in California.

Once you have an idea, there are hundreds of details to think about. Is the game for young children or older players? Is the game educational? Is it for one player or two? Perhaps it's an MMORPG (Massively multiplayer online role-playing game), such as *World of Warcraft*. In this type of game, hundreds of players from all over the world can play at the same time.

A good game idea doesn't have to have a story or characters. *Tetris* and *Candy Crush Saga* are both simple games that players love!

Making a Game: The Characters

If your video game idea includes characters, you will need to create them. A game's characters might be humans, orcs, aliens, robots, or animals. They could also be something completely new. For example, Pac-Man is one of the best-known video game characters of all time. He's just a simple yellow circle, however, with an eye and a big mouth.

Many video games include enemy characters. An enemy might be an evil wizard, a rotting zombie, or even an angry vegetable. You will decide how the enemy character looks and behaves. How will it attack the player? What special skills or weapons will it have?

To create a character's look and actions, a designer works with artists, animators, and coders.

Many games have a boss character that the player meets at the end of the game. This is an enemy that's bigger, more powerful, and more challenging to beat than the other enemies in the game.

A game may include tools that allow players to customize the characters. Players can choose a character's skin color, hairstyle, clothes, armor, weapons, and other gear.

Making a Game: Designing Levels

Most video games have different levels. Each level in a game may take place in a new environment. It will challenge the player with new skills to learn, enemies to overcome, and puzzles to solve. In some repetitive games, each new level looks similar, but it's harder or faster than the last. A video game may have just 10 levels or several hundred!

Video game designers, artists, and coders create maps of a game. A map can show the whole game world. Each level may also have its own map to show players what's to come.

Assets ▶ SampleScenes ▶ **Materials**

MauveSmooth   NavyDarkGrid   NavyDarkSmoo...   NavyGrid   NavySmooth   Orange

A video game designer may begin work on a level by sketching it on paper. Next, the designer or coder builds a gray or white box level on a computer. This is a basic version of the level. It includes no details, but it allows the designer, coders, and testers to test play the level.

If the designer's ideas work, the level is ready to be polished. Now, the artists and coders get to work creating the final version of the level.

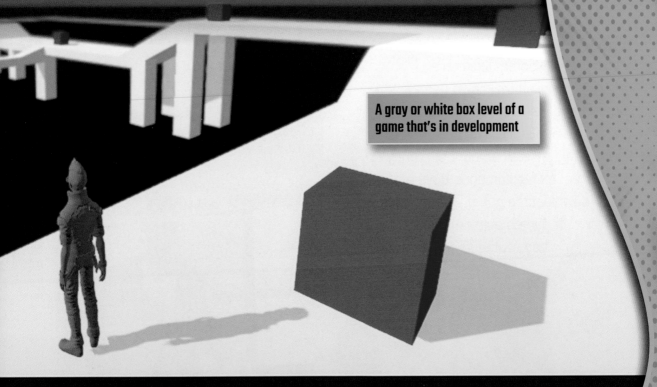

A gray or white box level of a game that's in development

ParticleClouds   PinkSmooth   SkyboxProcedu...   TealSmooth   TurquoiseSmoo...   WhiteSmooth   Ye

It's Gone Gold

Video game designers love creating games, but they still need to earn money from their work.

Once a designer has an idea, he or she may take it to a video game **publisher**. A publisher is a company that manufactures and sells games. If the publisher likes the idea, the company may pay the designer to produce the game. Then the designer will bring together a team of coders, artists, and other people to work on the game.

Some designers publish their own games and sell them online through an app store. The designer is paid a small amount of money each time someone buys and downloads a game. These types of games can sometimes be created in just a few days!

A video game designer gives a presentation called a pitch to a games publisher. During the pitch, the designer talks about his or her idea.

Some video game designers work for large publishing companies.

It can take two or three years for a large team to produce a realistic 3D action game. Finally, after thousands of hours of work, the game will be finished. When this happens, video game development teams say a game has "gone gold"!

Game fans play new games at the E3 Expo in Los Angeles. This is an event where games publishers launch and show off new games.

Designing the Future

The technology behind video games is developing fast. Something new is always just around the corner.

Today, some video game designers are working on games that can be played in virtual reality (VR). When a player wears a VR headset, the player feels as if he or she is actually inside the game's world. Many existing video games can't be played with this equipment. So new virtual reality games are needed for the future.

If you love playing video games, perhaps designing games will one day be your career. No one knows what the next big game will be or who will create it.

Perhaps it could be you!

A virtual reality (VR) Oculus Rift headset

Video game designer Ed McNeill works on his VR game *Darknet*, which can be seen on the computer screen.

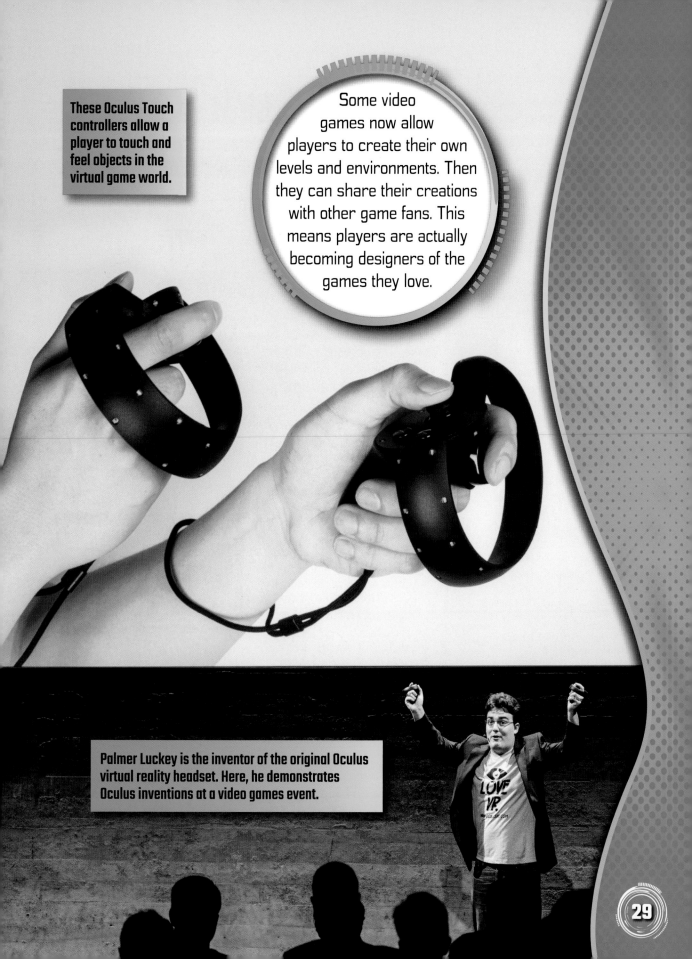

These Oculus Touch controllers allow a player to touch and feel objects in the virtual game world.

Some video games now allow players to create their own levels and environments. Then they can share their creations with other game fans. This means players are actually becoming designers of the games they love.

Palmer Luckey is the inventor of the original Oculus virtual reality headset. Here, he demonstrates Oculus inventions at a video games event.

Get to Work as a Video Game Designer

Q&A

What skills does a video game designer need?
You will need strong computer skills. Being good at art is also very helpful, but not essential. You will need patience, attention to detail, and good problem-solving skills.

What subjects should I study?
Computer science, math, art, and English. At a college or university, you can study computer science, video game design, graphic design, art, or animation.

How soon can I get started?
Today! Try writing your own games using the Scratch or Python programming languages. These online resources allow you to try coding and then share your creations with others. (Follow the link on page 32 to get to the Scratch and Python websites.) Find out if there's a coding club at your school or in your area and join up!

Where will I work?
You might work in the studio of a large publisher or a small development company. You might even set up your own company in your bedroom.

When will I work?
Creating a game is very hard work, and you will usually be working to a deadline. You may have to work until late at night and on weekends to get your work done. It's worth it, though, to produce a game that millions of gamers, just like you, will love!

Create a Game Design Document (GDD)

Once a video game designer has an idea, he or she creates a Game Design Document (GDD). A GDD is a detailed plan of everything that will be in the game.

Try thinking up an idea for a new video game. Then create a GDD that's filled with information about your idea. Your GDD can include text and drawings.

What's in a GDD?
- The story of the game
- The gameplay
- The objectives and rules
- The levels
- The characters

When working on your GDD, think about these questions:

- What does the game world look like? Is it a realistic, 3D world, or does it have a 2D, cartoon-style look?

- What does the player's character look like? What are the character's skills? What skill upgrades can a player earn? What items can a player collect, and how are they used?

- Who are the enemies? What do they look like, and what skills do they have? How does the player defeat the enemies?

- How many levels does the game have? What does each level look like? What challenges must the player overcome? How does the player win or complete the level? You can sketch out each level using a storyboard, like the one below.

- What kind of music will your game have? Listen to the music in the games you like. Is it happy or scary music? Does it help increase the tension as the game gets harder?

- What does the HUD (Heads-Up Display) system show? It might display, for example, the player's number of lives or how much fuel or time is left.

- What happens in the game's cutscenes? In a realistic, 3D game the cutscenes are like short movies that help tell the story for the player.

- What is your game called? Is it named after the game's world or a character, or does it have a dramatic or mysterious name?

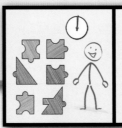

A storyboard

Glossary

3D (three-dimensional)
(three-di-MEN-shuh-nuhl) Having or appearing to have height, width, and depth.

animation (an-i-MAY-shuhn)
A technique that makes drawings, computer images, or 3D models move in a video game or movie.

artificial intelligence (AI)
(ar-ti-FISH-uhl in-TEL-uh-juhns)
Computer programs that allow computers to act or think for themselves.

avatar (A-vuh-tar)
An icon or character figure that represents a player in a video game.

code (KODE)
A language of letters, numbers, and symbols that is used to give instructions to a computer. A video game's code controls everything that happens in a game.

coder (KODE-ur)
A computer expert who writes the code for video games.

computer scientist
(kuhm-PYOO-tur SYE-uhn-tist)
A scientist who studies and develops computer software. Computer scientists study new ways in which computers can solve problems and be useful to people.

environment (en-VIRE-uhn-muhnt)
In a computer game, an area, such as an abandoned city or jungle, where the gameplay takes place.

genre (ZHAHN-ruh)
A type of book, movie, or video game. For example, horror, science fiction, and action are all types of genres.

industry (IN-duh-stree)
The businesses and companies that produce and sell a particular product.

inspiration (in-spuh-RAY-shuhn)
A source of ideas.

level (LEV-uhl)
In a video game, an environment or stage that the player tries to complete.

objective (uhb-JEK-tiv)
A goal to reach or a challenge to overcome.

program (PROH-gram)
To give a sequence of instructions to a computer so it performs a particular task. Also, the word for the sequence of instructions written by a computer programmer or coder.

publisher (PUB-lish-ur)
A company that produces and sells products such as video games, books, or magazines.

software (SAWFT-ware)
The programs that are used to operate computers.

sound effect (SOUND uh-FEKT)
A sound, other than music or voices, that is artificially created for a video game, movie, or TV show. For example, an explosion is a sound effect.

strategy (STRAT-uh-jee)
A plan of actions that helps a player win a game.

video arcade (VID-ee-oh ar-KADE)
A place where people can pay to play video games and other entertainment machines, such as pinball or pool.

Index

A
Angry Birds 10
animation 16–17, 22, 30
artificial intelligence 12
artists 10, 14–15, 16, 22,
    24–25, 26

C
Candy Crush Saga 10, 21
characters 5, 12, 14–15,
    16–17, 18–19, 22–23, 30
code 12–13
coders 10, 12–13, 19, 22,
    24–25, 26

D
Darknet 28
Douglas, Alexander S. 7

E
EDSAC computer 7
enemies 22, 24, 30

G
game engines 12

I
Iisalo, Jaakko 10

L
levels 10, 24–25, 29, 30
Luckey, Palmer 29

M
maps 24
McNeill, Ed 28
Minecraft 5, 10
MMORPGs (Massively
    multiplayer online
    role-playing games) 21
mobile app games 10–11, 26
modeling programs 14–15
motion capture 16–17

N
Nim 6
NIMROD computer 6
Nintendo Game Boy 9

O
Oculus VR equipment 28–29
OXO game 7

P
Pac-Man 9, 22
Pokémon 20
publishers 26–27

S
Sims, The 5
sound effects 12, 19
sound engineers 10, 18–19
Space Invaders 9
Spacewar! 8

T
Tajiri, Satoshi 20
testers 10, 18–19, 25
Tetris 21

V
video arcades 8–9
virtual reality games 28–29

W
World of Warcraft 5, 21
writers 10, 18–19

Read More

Jozefowicz, Chris. *Video Game Developer (Cool Careers: Cutting Edge)*. New York: Gareth Stevens Publishing (2010).

Wood, Alix. *Video Game Designer (The World's Coolest Jobs)*. New York: Rosen Publishing (2014).

Learn More Online

To learn more about video game design, go to:
www.rubytuesdaybooks.com/videogamedesigner